THE ANGEL WITHIN

Gayle,

Power

Bonnie
2025

The Angel Within: God, Angel, Me — As Being Human

ISBN: 9798558984989

A Publication of Tall Pine Books
|| tallpinebooks.com

*Printed in the United States of America

THE ANGEL WITHIN

GOD, ANGEL, ME — AS BEING HUMAN

BONNIE J. SCHAAL

Tall Pine

Again, this book can only be dedicated to my best friend, GOD.

SPECIAL THANKS

Thank you to all of you...daughters, L.U., MFR, J.N., P.M., you know who you are. Your help and knowledge for me and my endeavor to get this second book published is a great accomplishment. Again, thank you...

To my ever-so-patient S O, I love you, always, me... Your strength and understanding bring me joy every day. You know this, and I feel this. Thank you.

Most importantly, GOD, through your power and acknowledgement of this Angel to Human, can only be a God-given experience ... Thank you, I know my wings are waiting...

CONTENTS

PREFACE

To know oneself is for greater good

To know oneself through God is divine

To live through God is your best life

To be oneself through God's perfect life

Being perfect is a challenge we only can strive for

But as humans we don't get

Only through God, can we achieve the Spirit to do our best with God's help. We can be our best *us,* and this is perfect.

1

Today starts a new realm, a new day, new year, 2020. God again has "Picked Me," to do more of His encouraging and enlightening work. This is our second book.

As our first book has been called "God Picked Me," for reasons you will know when you read it. God has called me to write His words again.

This book is to be called, "The Angel Within."

It was on October 26, 2019 when my encounter with this message was brought to my dream. These encounters have taught me so much and I knew I had to be aware of their true meaning.

ENCOUNTER # 1

October 26, 2019

"The Angel Within"

Your wings are here and waiting,
Happy, smiling, content,
They are in this frame for safety,
Where no one can come and complain,
The day will come and they will be restored,
Upon your back again.
So go and find these words.
Share all you can,
Because, the day is coming soon,
To where you fly again.

3

At first I didn't know what to make of this dream. Was I going to die? Was I going to understand? But I did know these words were very important, so I had to listen and wait. On November 14, 2019, it became very clear to me the knowledge of these words.

It was not death.

It was freedom. Freedom from pain, knowledge, understanding. To know what freedom is. Free will, forgiveness, for others and self.

I get that. It made so much sense to me and I knew there was more to come. Not yet in the form of a new book, but I knew it was going to be worth the wait and understanding.

So I did.

4

ENCOUNTER # 2

December 11, 2019

Again in my dream on December 11, 2019 God woke me and told me to write.

> Love of Heart
> Beats till the end...
> Love of soul
> Is eternal...

5

ENCOUNTER # 3

December 15, 2019

God woke me again and told me to write.

"Love of Self is Always Unselfish."

6

When you are open to God's Word, you have a feeling that you have accomplished yourself and a calm of self reveals through you.

Wow, I'm still learning to be patient and wait for many revelations, as they are happening everyday.

The holidays have come and gone.

This new year has begun. I also knew I had some obstacles I had to clean up. In time things got resolved and this moment began.

ENCOUNTER # 4

January 11, 2020

I woke up screaming, calling, CLS, " I only have 3 to 4 weeks to live!"

My Dream: S O and I were at an event getting food. Breakfast to be specific. I left to find CLS, we were eating ice cream. I went back to find S O, he was gone. The breakfast was on the table. Other people were in the seats. S O's seat was empty. Then I was at a clinic, in a room. The person, a lady, white doctor coat on, short bleach blonde hair, dark, dark brown eyes, came and kissed my forehead and said, "Yes, 3-4 weeks to live." Then walked away. I chased after her, she opened a door, stood, then went behind the door and said "Yes, 3-4 weeks." She closed the door.

I tried to stop her from shutting the door. There was no handle. I couldn't open the door. She was gone. I screamed for CLS, yelling "3-4 weeks to live." I saw CLS and woke up.

K nowing what this dream means is exciting.

Death does not mean *die*. It means rebirth of a cycle, a new beginning. Start of a new plan, balance, development.

The #3 is Trinity, mind, body, spirit = harmony. This dream has a spiritual message.

The #4 is balance of energies with a partner. Growing in perfect balance.

Together they make #7

The #7 is a mystical number, marking beginnings and endings. Cycle period for growth and development. 7 Chakras, 7 heavens, 7 days of the creation of the world. Every 7 years is a death and rebirth of cycle.

This is exciting because I know I'm in a new cycle and am growing. Changing emotionally and spiritually.

My awakening in life to grow and regain new knowledge.

The heavens opening for my renewal, a rebirth of knowing, happenings, learning.

It is what God has been telling me and I have asked for.

For God's knowledge for me to understand.

Also, as a door closes another door opens.

When God shows you a door closed, leave it closed. In time another door opens, that one may go through.

9

As always my days are becoming more and more interesting. Receiving knowledge and listening are what I am to do. Open my ears and obey these words.

In my understanding I know I am part of a bigger world of God. As I wake each day God gives Me His pleasure and words of wisdom to share. This I know I must do.

Taking these words from God and trying to put them in human form is a trial in itself. Something I know I am chosen to do. I also am very happy to do this work.

It makes me feel like the world is changing, as it is every day. As we revolve around it. The world does not revolve around us. I know we would like to think that way, but actions are not to be revolving, think of it. Moving every day in a world that has been created to show humankind how wonderful our lives really are. The beauty of all things great and small, large and awesome. We get to live here. Enjoying this world's many facets and learning, for our greater good. But yes, we must learn, respect, believe, and show gratitude for this big expanse we call home.

10

ENCOUNTER # 5

Today I woke up to find that I had been dreaming (like I always do), of an old friend who passed away from cancer. In my dream I was singing. He was there to listen, and my pitch was perfect. The song "Only You," every word was correct.

As in many of my dreams this friend was laughing, smiling, happy. When the song was over. I looked at him and said, "Oh that's right, you are dead."
I woke up happy, knowing I saw my friend of over 50 years, happy and smiling, it made this dream even better.

The better connection in our dreams, they, most of the time reflect our daily life. Maybe something makes us realize, a change is needed, or a problem

has been solved. A lesson to be learned, or lesson to be changed. But in dreams we know what is on our mind as we enter sleep. With me, my dreams help me to come to a conclusion of what I am to learn, release, or knowledge to be understood.
As this one:

Male: Death: Friend: Singing: is great strength, power, ability.

can represent an old part dying and a new beginning.

Is something that you remember of that time a good or a bad memory. Is it happy, joy, praise, emotion?

So I feel my dream is meant for me to keep my path and my balance.

To move forward and keep gaining my strength and enlightenment of things to come and to stay focused on my journey.

Balance in our lives is very important to us daily. We all have had bad, crazy, wrong feelings through our days, our lives. To understand these is so important to us. To realize everyone needs guidance and help at some time. It is necessary to be able to keep our focus and our balance. To know ourselves, and to know just what we need to keep us going. We can teach ourselves to be happy, sad, mean, or any emotion.

To teach ourselves to find the beauty in all, is a very hard lesson. We are humans, and humans lack discipline, structure and balance. I say this all the time, "We need to be our best advocates for our own self."

We live in these bodies and we are the ones to know ourselves best. Our bodies tell us our true feelings. How we want to learn is another aspect. We can choose to do so, or we can choose not to.
In my experience I choose to learn. It has been hard and I have been stubborn and difficult with myself at times. That stubbornness didn't work to my benefit or my balance.

As for me, I do try to move forward.

Knowing the difference in feeling balanced and not, can and will spoil your day, your being. I encourage you to find yours. It really does help make a difference. Remembering, moving forward is the best. The past is past. Good, bad, indifferent, we still get to choose what direction to go. Think before you choose. Take 10 seconds to breath, or more. Move in your best balance for you. Always you. God, if you ask Him and let Him, will always give you your greater path.

11

Today is another obstacle week. Learning much information and figuring how to use this for my best and balance. This came to me in a very unusual way, but I must remember to:

Be magnanimous.

Be trustful

Be hopeful and

be patient.

I have been saying this for days and putting it to use. It is so helpful to clear my head and see how this saying is useful to my balance. God has been telling me and talking to me through many words and I take this to my core. I know how to listen. This doesn't mean I always do. But when I don't, I get bit in the ass. Things change, I stop my energy, and balance is out of sync. I know you understand as we all feel when the universe is out of whack in our lives. Thank You God for pulling me back to earth and making me stand tall.

Another good verse is:

"Organize your life around your dreams, and watch them come true."

This has been a lifeline in my life. Many times I have had to do this. In my last book "God Picked Me," my encounters have been my dreams and the truth to much of me being alive. They have shown me that when I am learning and listening MIRACLES happen. Yes, I do believe in miracles. I AM that miracle. As I always want these miracles. Writing is a Miracle. Being published is a Miracle. Being able to understand all of this is a Miracle. At least to me it is.

12

Today is Valentine's Day, February 14, 2020, Friday. A day of passion for all. Even though it is a "holiday" of love. Think of it as a day to *love yourself*. To put yourself first and use this respect for your own enjoyment. Respect of self is a very big commitment to self. We all need to have this commitment for our greater good.

As God has told, shown and proven to me, many times, as I have needed this reminder.

"LOVE OF SELF IS ALWAYS UNSELFISH"

We need to remember to love ourselves. If we cannot love ourselves, how do we learn to love each other. Or to love other things, like animals and this beautiful world that God created to bless us. I am reminded of this often, especially when I am hard on myself, as I fall short in my daily life. Or sometimes, I just believe I fall short. God has proven to me time and time again this earth is of human agenda, time, and realm. It was put here for our enjoyment. It is our place and time to learn the lessons that we each need for our growth. To learn our path on our journey through this age of life, and to do our best, not just for ourselves, but to be examples for the generations to come.

It is sad to me to see this new generation be so selfish and all about "ME, ME, ME." One day they will be accountable for these wayward paths in the judgment of our creator. In my faith I say "God." That is a very scary thing to have to think about. Judgment of past, present, future. Rights, wrongs, selfishness of my/our creation. Thank You God for forgiving me, this human of conscious mind and body. Every day I remind myself to be thankful of God's love for me. To say thank You God for all of my glad, happy, sad, wrong events. I created each of them my way. As I am the only one who can accept my own responsibility for them. No one has told me to do this or that. Me, just me. Wow, ouch, that just got to me. But as always, Thank You God.

I will try and strive to do better. I have the tools to do this, as it is a gift to cherish and trust. God does not make junk. God does not make imperfect. We humans make imperfect things. Yes, another lesson. One we all can and should learn. Again, thank You God.

13

Today again, I woke up with my eyes open. Thank You God. I am celebrating my two years of FREEDOM FROM CANCER. I'm still on my infusion of Keytruda, every three weeks, my immunotherapy treatment. "Keep my cancer away," through the help of my own body with Keytruda.

This is a big achievement in cancer treatment. I know without my miracles of survival and God making this happen, I would not be alive today. As shared in my other book, "God Picked Me," I am this miracle, and am able to celebrate two years of freedom from cancer. It was a rocky road with many trials to walk through to get here today.

All that I accept, all that I had to go through. Not to say I didn't complain, and ask at times "Why me?" but again, " Why not me." As I went through cancer I learned more coping skills and control of myself, and how without my faith, my God, I would not have survived. This I know for sure. People, many people, prayed for me and my struggle. Without all these prayers, I also know this miracle of my life wouldn't have happened. Thank you all for your loving prayers. Please, keep them coming, as I am asking again, I always need and receive them. I feel them every day. Thank you.

ENCOUNTER # 6

February 14, 2020

Love with Soul
Spirit thru God
Hope in Heart
"Trilogy"

In my dream of February 14, 2020 as God said these words and told me to write them down. I understood what He meant.

1. Love with Soul:
You can't have love without your soul. Your soul is love.

2. Spirit through God:

Is your spirit working for your good? Spirit is only through God.

3. Hope in Heart:
Is the last thing you lose. Your hope in your heart.

15

What a way to start the day. A trilogy to remember words so profound that stop and make you think. Words to give your day a boost. Yes, a boost. When you think about words some really resonate within you and others we discard as not important. But all words bring something. They may be so minor, as we think about them, but really all words matter. A lesson I have learned, and am still learning.

We say words to express our feelings, our love, our sorrow, our anger, our contentment, our values, our minds. We are taught the correct words as children to understand daily life. We listen and learn from words.

I wonder why it is so hard for all humans to listen to the Word of God and actually hear.

These words also tell me the meaning of daily life. How life happened, how life became, how words hurt and destroy. To think about that is a big part of knowledge we learn. Just take a moment to think in your own mind and recount many instances when words cut us to the quick, or we said harsh words. Scary isn't it?

Though we may have had those days, we can still say words are very important. We could not live without the use and understanding of words. Okay, enough lessons for today.

Don't take words for granted. Think before you speak. Use your words well.

16

Today is Monday. Thank goodness this weekend is over. It was a weekend of beautiful weather. Timing, perils, and obstacles. As the saying goes, "whatever could go wrong, did." Things sometimes just don't go as planned. We think our methods are sound but they turn out to be all wrong. One thing I have to school myself on is *listening to my gut*. People when your gut is telling you "NO, not a good idea!" LISTEN. I wish I had. But, should-a, could-a, would-a, is past. As the days progressed, I did listen to that little voice inside me and all things changed and worked for my good. The outcome became a good end to a bad start. I'm always confused by this at first, but as I trusted God, and His words of understanding, all became clear and my outcome became perfect. Not to say I wasn't sweating bullets during the disaster, but in the end I came to understand if I had only listened to God's Words or if you choose to say, *my gut*, this would have been a much easier outcome from the start. My words resounded in my ear...

Be trustful.

Be hopeful.

Be patient.

Time and time again these words "catch me and win." So again, I took them to heart and stood steadfast and became a winner. Thank You God, for showing this human again, that You are in control.

Also going through this phase my good friend, CWR, came to my mind, and hearing her words of encouragement over and over again made this time more stable. As humans we don't have much patience. At least my patience is dull. We need to see the good and have patience. Yes, that feels uncomfortable, but necessary, as the saying goes.

PATIENCE IS A VIRTUE

Wow, did I need this one. When I talk to God, patience is not one quality I ask for. This, I have learned the hard way. Don't ask, don't receive. But in all things, sometimes it's needed and given whether you asked or not. So, all in all, this weekend was a good one and I thank God for His perfect outcome in my life. As I am, "a human work in progress." Always moving forward trying to find my path on this long journey of life.

So again I say, "Thank You God it's Monday, a beautiful day."

17

Today is a day of facts. The fact is I opened my eyes this morning. Another fact is, I am breathing. I can walk. I am healthy. I am blessed.

Yes, I am a cancer survivor. I have had three bouts of cancer, all the same kind. Endometrial/cervical, in my female parts. Pelvic region, liver and bowel. Different times. Ranging from 1995-2017. My biggest span was 1995-2015. I was getting ready to celebrate my 20th year of staying clean of cancer, when the nasty cell became reality and came back. 20 years, this is not supposed to happen. But it did. FACT. In my other book "God Picked Me" that is all about my survival. How God's many miracles saved my life with my wonderful team, family, friends, pray'ers, supporters and of course my amazing doctors. I only survived because of this team, and our will to see me live.

As I said, this is a day of facts.

That is a big one. I am still in treatment for this cancer. Getting my Keytruda, (immunotherapy drug) to keep the cells away, working with my body's immune system to keep me healthy. I love that I am able to do God's work again. Finding His words to put on paper, to tell His story of this amazing person, yes *me*, who is willing to be His servant. Yes, I will do this every time He asks. I come as a human, and powerless without God's hand on my life. I have been taught to hear and listen to these facts of which I speak. Words of wisdom, strength, knowledge and clarity. I understand, because I have, and am willing. This is a fact in my life today, every day, I choose to follow. I cherish this and I accept this challenge for me. I would encourage you, all of you, to accept it as well. My life is not a cupcake, full of cherries and whip cream. But, the fact is I have those days when it is.

FACT, we are humans, living, breathing, we have freedom of choice. We have the choice to say YES and NO. But, it is always our own to choose. Again that is FACT.

I am writing today to show that FACT is a positive word. God wants us to be in a positive frame of mind and believe the facts that are presented before us. Facts of finding truth in our daily life and bringing forth that which is in our being to be that fact. Honesty, truth, trust, love, forgiveness, hope, splendor, compassion, wisdom, the list goes on. Find in ourselves what we wish for others. Gifts to ourselves that we give to others. Yes, my friends, these are God's FACTS.

So as we go along our day today and smile, laugh, be in our day, remember to know the facts and use the facts *for you.* Yes, FACTS...

18

I n my journey, life, path, I try to make my way as comfortable as I can. God's grace for me makes this for my understanding and freedom. I have talked about this many times, in many ways, and the ways of why it is important.

One way for me is by prayer to God and also His angels, sent to help, secure, comfort. I know in my life, without my angels, I am alone. I call on them daily. I pray to them, and with them. You can call them by name, (some do have names) or just by saying "my angel." I know I have many.

In a recent book I have read the sentence said, "God has many angels, some 144,000." Some are unnamed and some have very specific names. I try to use these names, as I also call on the unnamed angels. I feel so empowered to be able to use these spirits of God for my daily comfort. Thank You God for giving these gifts to this human. As a human I like to think I am gifted to receive knowledge through God's spiritual guidance and angels. I can feel this power through my being and hold steadfast to these truths. This big universe is ours to put in our lives in the aspect that best fits our comfort. I am comforted by saying angels. You may call them as you choose.

Every day my angels and I have very intricate conversations. Conversations that I am able to listen, to understand, comprehend and learn. I try my best to be the best me I can. Oh boy, that is not easy.

Daily life is very distracting and takes a lot of time to walk through every day. We have good days and we have bad days. But at least we have these days. Knowing faith is part of daily life helps me to walk my path. In my other book "God Picked Me" I told of an encounter #8, I had about being God's angel. That my path about becoming human from angel was going to be "hard." Yet, that is what I chose. Yes, this path has been hard, but it also has been miraculous. It took me 60 plus years to find this truth and learn how to deal with it. I'm not at all disappointed about my journey. I'm excited to know how I became. I'm excited to know I was the chosen one to do God's work. I'm not a scholar, I'm not an expert. What I am is accepting of God's truth and always wanting to know. From a small age, I knew value in humans. I knew we were here on earth to make wonderful things happen. To learn, to explore, and to chart the impossible. But as with God, NOTHING is impossible. I get more disappointed when I feel I have not understood or didn't listen well to my truth. I live a wonderful life. I accept this to be true for me. To be able to speak God's word. To take these words, put them on paper, and present them to humans. That is a beautiful day.

19

Angels, if we let them, want to guide us along the path of righteousness. We all do feel this in our hearts. We know when this is good or this is bad. Our hearts ache. If you choose it, the good or bad, that angel's sitting on each shoulder waiting for you to choose who will win. Of course, we want good to always win. But we are humans and have the power of choice. So we choose and hope we have chosen the best for our paths, our balance. Because we all know when we have made the wrong choice. It hurts, it scares, it just doesn't feel true. Wow, how many times have each of us felt this. I can't even count. I'll just say *many*. Yes *many*, as we move on and knowledge allows, we grow to know the difference. We are able to discern the difference of doing the thing that feels good, or the thing that feels terrible. As the innocence of a child wears off, and we become adults we are supposed to know better. Ha, ha, on us. Again we have had the choice to make and choose. Free will.

What a wonderful life lesson to be able to choose. I will never say I did not have the freedom to choose. Yes, I had my time in life to be respectful of my parents, elders, those in charge, and I was taught to be respectful. Didn't always mean I liked it, but we did it. That goes along with learning morals, values, and concepts. Learning to become us. We all need teachers. We all need lessons in learning. What we all have is the choice in what we want to make part of our person. Our being, our us. Our own path in the journey of life. To be our own person to live our own life. We are responsible for our life. We are responsible for every aspect of our daily time on this earth. No one can blame someone else for our wrong teaching. We have the power to be better and to learn a different way, path, or concept. What we must do is learn, understand and make that happen for ourselves. NO ONE is to blame for our own choices. Remember that. We need to accept our choosing. Only us, ourselves. "FREE WILL." We get to choose the end result.

Not to say bad doesn't happen, and that some *bad* is not of our choosing. But, how we react is our choosing. How we, in turn, take that bad and make it work for our good. Yes, this is for us to do. This world is not humanly perfect. So yes, we are in the midst of imperfection. Again, FREE WILL. What we do to make bad into good is our choice. Taking bad, and making it worse, that can be your choice. Taking bad and making it good, is again your choice. We have been taught to choose wisely. To accept this choice. So I say, please think and make your choice a wonderful lesson for you, in your wonderful life.

Ask these angels, teachers of choice, to intervene and help to make you understand yourself. The *you,* you are meant to be. "THE ANGEL WITHIN" who lives in all of us, humans.

Thank you Angels. Thank You God.

20

I am looking at this beautiful world today. The sky is so blue, the clouds are puffy, fluffy. I feel I could jump from one to another. The sun is shining, glowing. Making me smile. I'm feeling the power of my angels, my guardians, my friends. God reminded me of a verse I had been told to write down a while ago. One that came to me in one of my dreams. Wow, Thank You God, again.

Come to Me with open arms, My arms will always be there, Come to Me and hold Me tight, My arms will never fail.

Sometimes when I'm feeling needy or just lonesome I think of this verse. It calms me, It warms me, it comforts me. I know these words are for my heart to smile and know God loves me. This I do know for sure. This I know I can count on. This I just know. Thank You God.

Having happy days is what God wants for our lives. God wants us to know all days can be happy, fulfilling, complete. I want this and do my best to accomplish this daily event. I want you to know you can also.

Give yourself your *you*. Release *you* to the world. Smile at your accomplishments. Be proud and happy for you. Take time and see how you in turn see your day. Your heart is smiling for your best you.

Happy you, the angels heaven sent this message for. All angels are our guardians.

21

A long way back, I was a young girl. A girl who didn't know who she was. A girl who didn't understand who or why she was in this life. I was not gifted in school. I was not gifted at spelling, reading, or math. I saw many words, numbers, letters, backwards. So school and I were only to get through. It was a struggle, but I knew I would be okay. I knew life had many accomplishments for me. I learned to ice skate, and did it well. I learned horseback riding, and I did my best. I loved those horses. They were my friends . We learned to be partners. All through that, school still was difficult for me. I did my best. I graduated and moved forward.

My life became my best for me. I got married and had children, all the requirements. It was when my child was diagnosed with dyslexia that I found I had been dyslexic as well. So all my years of not knowing this, I was called dumb, stupid, inept. Well that takes its toll. You believe it yourself because you don't know any different. We took this to heart. I got help for my child and me and learned how to cope. Another life lesson.

Nowadays these things are learned, they are in your DNA. Okay. I can accept this. I just hate that it's something that gets passed along. But as we learned, we can overcome it. We can learn to work through the stigma. We did. And today it is okay for all of us.

I had to learn to accept myself and know that I am not dumb, I am not stupid. Teachers of all kinds are there to help. I am one of my teachers. I am one of my helpers. We all are able to help others as we help ourselves. God's gift to me has proven this many times. Every day, every decision I make, I am my teacher. This world has grown and realized people are human, and humans can learn and need to be taught. What makes it easier is that I know I want this help and I know God has been my support all the time. My life is blessed. I have wonderful people who share my time on this earth. My children, my friends, my people. Thank you all. My S O is one. He is a champion for me. He always tells me how smart I am. How he loves my logic and problem-solving methods. He is always encouraging for my greater good. We work well together. That makes us equal. This makes us a pair, couple, and partners. We are strong together. Thank you S O, I love you always.

I know God put us together for our greater life, our greater good. As I'm alive today, and working for tomorrow, I will always say, *Thank You God.*

22

Another three weeks have passed, Keytruda time. My body sure does tell me when it's time for this infusion, it's ready. I also go see my oncologist. I had an event at my last Keytruda, three weeks ago. All went well with the infusion (treatment). As nurse A, put the needle in my port and started the drip, I could feel the Keytruda pulsing through my veins. This wasn't new to me, I have felt this before. For the 40 minute drip all was okay, then as nurse A was putting the cleanse solution through to clear the last of the Keytruda in my vein, I felt my finger-tips get needles and pins. My tummy got nauseous, and I felt tipsy. This was a feeling I remembered from past chemotherapy. I was supposed to go run errands, but went home as I didn't feel well. At home I was very nauseous and felt ill, so I went to lay down, and I slept for hours and woke up feeling slightly better, but still off. I got through the day and 24-hours later I was okay.

This is the reason for seeing my oncologist at this appointment. We checked in with my routine to make sure all things are working for my good. We say our usual "hellos" and I tell him of this event. I had thought that maybe I was getting a bug coming on, and that was the cause. When I heard Dr. N say the same, I was relieved he felt the same as I did. The amazing part is that I agreed with him, and the true message is that Keytruda was doing its job with my body's immune system to kill the cells that would cause an illness. I was fighting these attackers to clean my body of illness as Keytruda and my immune system were a team for my good. How great is that? Exactly what was supposed to happen. Now I know Keytruda is for my benefit and working well with my immune system. Wow, I have been on Keytruda for 2 1/2 years now. Fighting cancer cells in my body and also anything else to attack me internally. How great is that? Thank you Keytruda. Thank You God.

Now on to get my normal treatment today. All went well, I did my 40 minutes, had a good infusion, and went on my way. No events, so I am certain that the last infusion event was that I was starting to become ill. Keytruda did its job killing those bad cells and pushing my immune system to fight as a team in my body. I'm alive, I'm breathing, I'm good to go for another three weeks. Again, another one of God's miracles in my life. "Keytruda." Thank You God, this child of yours is very grateful.

23

Coronavirus - Covid-19

We, in today's news and world, are worried about the spread from around the world. Started in China and now the *world panic* has started.

"It's the end of the world!"

We have had others, flus, viruses, elements before. Yes this is a bad one and many are being caught up in this health scare. Some have or will die, some are just sick. It is an outbreak of an illness. There are many that happen. These get spread as people do not take precautions and forget to mind health regulations. Be vigilant and make hygiene extra special. Do the extra step. Wash your hands, cover your mouth when you sneeze, cough, etc.

A germ is a germ. You can spread your germs anywhere. Be sensitive to your fellow human and cover your face. Give the tissue and make it your priority to cover you.

Don't shake hands or give that kiss. Be polite and give that greeting with a smile or a nod. Don't touch each other at this time. This too will pass. Ailments don't stay around forever. Be your best advocate for you. You are responsible for your own human body. When you love your body you are loving your neighbor. Understand we all carry germs in our everyday life. We touch everything. Remember to wash your hands. They are germ carriers and need protection too. Don't touch your face, mouth, eyes. Go and wash. Clean your surfaces and your body. As God has said, "Your body is your temple." Keep it clean. Don't infect others with your germs. Wash, and all will be restored.

God promises this world for us to enjoy. So enjoy. As being mindful of our surroundings, Keep it clean. Make it our temple to worship. Make it our routine to resurface the old and make new again.

Please just wash your environment, your space, your body, your hands. May God bless us all. Thank You God.

24

God gave us life to be humans in this world. What have we done? We work all the time. The need for things has become greater than our love of life. It is all about me, me, me... I want, I will take, I will get. No matter what. Yes, we are to enjoy. Yes, we are supposed to enjoy our life. But take a second and look, listen, and see. We have not done this as much as we were trained. So stop and look, listen, see, this great universe. Be an active part of now. Take a break. Stop your device. Stop your face in tunnel vision. Stop your *not allowing you to be you.* Now God is calling. Answer that call and say yes to be a bigger part of today, now, tomorrow. Our children need us to slow down and teach them the slower pace of life. Please hear these words for our health and lives.

Look at the sky, see the clouds moving? The shapes in your imagination, be that child again. Ask God to open your heart . To show you the way. Stop being so grumpy, short tempered, angry. I can promise you, if you do you will see a difference In you and your surroundings, and even in the people you touch.

Be softer spoken. Less in a rush. Make time for smelling the roses. Take that vacation. Whether you stay at home or travel. It's your vacation to just *be and enjoy.* Earth smells great. Flowers, trees, grass, it all has a beautiful smell. All living things have their own smell.

So do it. Enjoy it. Take that break and go outside and breathe. Deep in your lungs. Feel that heat go into your body and then exhale. Now do it again.

See that wasn't so bad? I beg you to do this as much as you can. Life is too short not to. Things happen. Don't miss them. They are important. For you and yours as well, as all human breathing life.

25

Did you wake up today? I did, and I am breathing. I can see, I can do all. Thank You God.

Just think of how wonderful this world is. Just think how every day we humans are being treated to life. As we take for granted the normal everyday routines.

Life as of now has stopped. We have a virus among us and it is causing panic and havoc all over the world.

As God says "rest in me," take hope and blessings for you know all is under control and going to be okay. We have had these world viruses, sicknesses, and troubles before. Ten years ago it was Swine Flu, I had it. It went from the flu, into bronchitis, and then walking pneumonia. I was sick for almost 3 months. It passed. I'm fine and I have not had the flu since. That's 10 years. I do not get a flu shot, my choice. I have learned to allow my body and my immune system to work together for my good.

Not to say I haven't had cancer and am still fighting to keep my cancer in line. I do get my immunotherapy treatments that work with my body as well. So all in all, I am pretty well in my immune system mode. Study your immune system of your own body and you'll learn a lot about yourself. Take the time to teach you how you work. These are life lessons for you. Learning about our bodies and the function of our own body is one of our needed teachings for our life. We must learn when we need to do better for ourselves. As we do this, it also teaches us to help others and show compassion toward our fellow man, neighbors, friends, family. We all need each other to sustain life on this wonderful earth. This is our world. We need to take care of us, so we can take care of the universe. God created this for us. Humans, animals, all living breathing to consume life. If light does not exist, the sun, nothing could live. If air, wind, breeze, didn't happen... nothing would move. Without trees, flowers, and various plants, many animals and humans could not exist. All would perish. All would be dead.

Take a moment and think about this and remember to look to the surroundings. See this beautiful expanse and do your best to be a part of a happy necessary world for all of us. Take part in her survival. Because we need her in order to survive.

Have a blessed day and be a part of knowing you are a needed part of today, of the universe, of life.

26

Oh my, God is so good. He protects and gives knowledge when the correct time is in place. Today, Sunday, a glorious day, beautiful sun, sky, warmth, to realize my dream of January. My eyes are finally open to this knowledge of what this dream means.

"3-4 weeks to live"

It is about this trying time. To see the events of these days. To remind myself and be aware of my "social distancing." To keep clear of interaction and protect my body, surroundings, where I am, who I'm with, or I could be in trouble. As I have had a compromised immune system, cancer, so interaction with many people had to stop. I had to protect myself to keep me cancer free and be on my road to stay this way . We all miss the interaction but we need to be mindful of others and heed the warnings of group togetherness. It's our safety that is a must.

Thank You God. I get it. I'm alive and so are you . Let's keep it this way.

27

These days of being contained have given me much time to reflect and think and pray. Our world needs a lot of prayer. We need a lot of healing. We are not perfect humans. We take for granted so many of God's comforts, and we destroy this beautiful world. Yes I am included, we all must try better to believe we can make a difference. Pray to whom you choose. Pray for our humanity, our lives, our freedoms, our choices.

As I always do, I dream. My dream was just going in circles. Seeing the same scene over and over. Three times to be exact. Trying to get somewhere but starting over each time at the same spot. Ending at the same spot. To understand I have to make changes in my life, so I don't end up in the same spot over and over again. Yes I'm trying and sometimes I do. But I always keep trying.

Give yourself more credit for the things you complete, accomplish and finish. This doesn't mean "all at once," but rather, finish what you start. Look at what you did and be proud of yourself for getting it finished. I'm learning to do this. I will do this. Look at myself, yourself, for your own gratification. You did it. Be glad, happy, encouraged.

Times are tough. Try not to have the attitude "poor me." We are all together to make a difference. God is showing me, "why not me," and I get that. But I won't sink in it. I will power through and make it better for me and others. That is what life is about. Your path, your journey, your betterment.

28

God has always taught me we are all angels. We have different jobs and our spirit comes in different forms. I do and am a believer in "The Angel Within." It is our job to see and listen to our bodies to figure out who and what our inner angel is telling us. How to work with our angel and do the best for us as a pair.

It brought me great comfort to realize I was wanting to learn of this human life. To leave my wings in God's great hands and become human. It was at my asking and my choosing to be a previous human and learn how to work with my inner Angel. As a child I knew this. Children are so accepting of the spirit realm and the spirits around them. They can and do teach us a lot. As we get older, our teen years, we lose a lot of our spiritual awareness. We learn to use our free will, and we disobey what is right in front of us. I will say it's okay. It's all part of growing up and making decisions in this human life. Learning right from wrong and deciding if we want to obey. Boy, was that a teacher. As I have had my teen years. Wow. But to my relief, I learned to pick and choose pretty well. Not all the time, but I'm 68 years old now. I've had many trials and made many mistakes, but again, it's all part of growing. Ouch! I have disappointed many, and I was disappointed too! Again, more learning.

Life never promised a bowl of cherries. We had to pick the bad and discard, to be able to eat the sweet. I really hope these lessons become a reality for many. As we learn it's never too late and we can adapt. Please remember to do your part, walk your path. Smell the air, eat the fruit, you are always on a journey and you have choices of your free will. Be kind, gentle, brave, be that "Angel Within."

29

We as a country, and as a world, have been on quarantine. Staying home. For weeks, months, trying to defend against this virus, Covid-19. I hope people are adhering to this new type of rule, at least for now.

I myself have been in isolation for over three weeks as I write this chapter. My choice, as I have a compromised immune system. Cancer. Getting my Keytruda to keep my body and cells at bay. Keeping myself at a large distance from you and from all. I'm hating every day, but I know it has to be done. Thank you great friends, family, for doing my shopping, gathering my needs, so I do not have to go myself and possibly come into contact with this dreaded virus. Your concern for me goes above and beyond. You are my separation from the outside world, and I thank you.

I love my porch, to be able to breathe fresh salt air and watch the waters, birds, boats, all passing by. It helps to know the world is still revolving and nature is in full spring. Chirping of birds, flowers in bloom, movement around, ahhhh, but yes, the lack of people moving about. People are exercising, running, walking, bicycling, not as groups but still moving. I take my walks, see my neighbors, keep my distance as required. We are all on *"wait and see."* Do what is necessary and be vigilant about personal space.

I can say it is working and many are welcome in this challenge. For our own safety. Thank You God. We have free will and are choosing well. Please be kind, generous, steadfast. This too shall pass. This is our time to be aware of the things we forget in our daily life. To stop and smell the roses. To give this world a break. The scientists are saying it is making a difference. The noise pollution and smog are reduced in many places where people are now seeing the sun and clouds. I hope this is true. The sky looks lovely to me, but I always think the sky is beautiful. Blue, with clouds and the smell of fresh air. Not to be taken advantage of in any way or any day. I just love to see and smell and hear. So I'm happy to be able to do this for as many days as I am able. Hoping it's every day of my life. Again, Thank You God.

Realizing life can be taken in a second, a minute, a day. As I have had to face this with cancer. Knowing my Keytruda, (immunotherapy) drug is part of my survival. It helps me every day. All day. Without it is the unknown for me. I am so grateful. As I will choose to be and do my best in many ways and challenges in the daily way called life.

30

Happy Easter Sunday 2020. "He has Risen."

Today Jesus has risen from the tomb. He has shown all God's great power and strength to be alive again and spoken to all. Every Easter since I am alive, my teachings have been about rebirth. My lessons are about the Trinity. Father, Son, Holy Spirit.

"God, Jesus, Spirit"

I have always been a believer in the Trinity. My upbringing, lessons, and my faith always included the Trinity.

The most special 3-point triangle that I know. In my childhood it was so easy to put my faith in this. Even when I really didn't understand its true meaning, I just believed. I did as I was taught and moved on. As a teen, well, that was more difficult. As teens we all had many difficult decisions to make and live by. At early 20 – 30 – 40 – many of my early lessons came back to me. I had children and it was my job to help them learn. To try to teach them that the Trinity was a belief they should be aware of. Some do and some have their own way and belief. As we are supposed to come into our own and believe our own way. God shows in time, our custom, our value. It's all according to our own understanding and our desire to understand. As God says, "He will never give us more than we can handle." I do know this to be true. I have always believed this throughout my life, as I still do to this day. God - Jesus - Spirit . I call on all of them to help me understand my life. Each has shown me protection, grace, mystery, clairvoyance, law, gratitude, more than I can list.

Each function is different. Ask, and you yourself will come to understand exactly what I am referring to. Truth, love, learning, understanding. Give yourself the power to do so. Open up your heart to let in this trinity and be filled with these blessings to be yours for the rest of your life. You will come to understand the meanings you are too. As with my faith in my Trinity I do. You are reading me talking about this, as God is my best friend, that is my truth. My choosing. My belief. I always call on God for my needs. I also ask Jesus and the Holy Spirit to clarify for me too! In my life, we all work for my/our human good. My human wellness, my human strength. As I ask and receive. TRY IT. I hope you like what you ask. As always remember, it is what you asked. Your choice. You alone have this choice. Again, this is your responsibility, because you made your choice. As in asking for anything, in all things, you alone have made this your choosing. You know the saying "be careful what you wish for, you just might get it." So choose wisely, be picky, be precise, be confident.

God loves us humans more than we can ever know. God made us. Remember Adam – Eve, family, this is where all human life began. This became God's gift to life on earth. We humans are the reason for many Easter lessons of life. To live, to die, to rise again for our good, our rebirth, our belief, our trust. To believe we are made of God's love, to create a better human world for all to achieve greatness.

Happy Easter Sunday 2020.

31

I t's very early in the morning, and I am so awake. I wish I were asleep! I'm not rested and I feel a bit tired. But in reality, I'm awake. My sleep is over. My thoughts get the best of me many times and it is so frustrating. Darkness is still around me. I hear the birds beautiful songs and life again has begun a new day. Time to begin. As the morning light rises and shines bright many clouds are soaring about. The sun is making many rays through the whisper of cloud cover. Good morning day.

My thoughts are through these times in this new normal time. Covid-19 is still among us. We are at "stay home," stay safe. But, I go back to my original feeling, one I have had for months. Well before this virus became our new normal. I said this, feel this, am living this.

"GOD IS PISSED"

God IS pissed. We humans have been put in lockdown, in our homes, with our families, our children, loved ones, pets.

Can you say you remember a time when the only people you are looking at every day is YOUR family unit.

I can, as life many years ago was about the family unit. It was so much different than today. In my years, most moms stayed at home. They took care of the house, the children, and the family. We all managed to live simpler. It was cheaper, but expensive, we didn't have as many THINGS. This is the way things were at that time.

As in every generation, that NORMAL life changes. Family life changes. People change. It happened to our parents, our grandparents, to us, and now to our children, and to some of our grandchildren. Again a new normal. Everyone is in a hurry. We are gathering more, spending more, working more, sleeping less, spending less time together. Wow, do you see it? That is why I have said,

"GOD IS PISSED"

Families are not together, someone is always on the go. Running here and there. Working to make ends meet. Getting children to activities, or lessons, or just where they feel they need to be.

Life has become separate. You go here, I'll go there. You do this, I'll do that, kids do... Can you see why I say, GOD IS PISSED.

We humans have lost our unity of family. I get it. I've done it too! Shame on all of us. We have forgotten family. I'm at fault. I'm in this stigma. I'm part of this outcome. OUCH!

I can't tell anyone what to do, I have a hard enough time dealing with myself, but I will suggest that you stop, take a breath and look, listen, feel this burden we have put upon ourselves.

Think about what you miss. Listen to what you don't hear, look at what you don't see. We have been put to a halt. Everything has stopped. We are staying home. Care for yourself, your family, your needs.

Do you get this? Do you feel the pull? Do you hear the silence?

Not so many cars on the move. Transportation is still, only the necessary continues.

You are allowed to grocery shop. You are allowed medical. You are allowed family.

Can you see the value? Feel the necessity. Hear the calm.

Yes, people are in watchful times. Jobs have stopped, only "essential" continue. No running here and there. As we have been told, take a walk, go exercise, walk your pets. Hunker down. Be in your homes, be with your family, help the elderly. Check on your neighbor. Keep your distance.

Can you see what is happening YES, "GOD IS PISSED."

So my question is? "DID GOD GET YOUR ATTEN-TION?" Please stop. Please think. Please listen. Please believe.

32

I stop and reread my chapters very often. It helps me to get into the next one and write again.

I have no idea sometimes what my pen will put on paper. What I do know is, this is OUR book. It is not only my thoughts, it is God's way of getting attention, using me, this human, to convey His words. God has taught me, I am His angel to use, to make what God wants to be learned, said, written. I almost feel like a person in a trance. Being led to pen and paper for a greater good. Yes, I will perform this. Yes, I will always say "yes" to God. I have been one of God's miracles, I am God's miracle. I am alive. I did my job. I lived through cancer. I worked hard to heal. I allowed this human body to recover. All because God told me to. I am sure you may think I'm eccentric, but that's okay, I've heard it all. So if I am, I'm good with that. But one thing I can say is, I am a believer. I am alive, I breathe, I woke up this morning.

I pray, I learn, I listen, God has many humans in this world. His many angels to perform His daily lessons for human reality. During my life I've always felt this. I've said "yes."

When God speaks, I get real joy to know I am allowed to understand this value in God's words to try to help humankind grow. Every day is a new chapter in all of our lives and we humans, if we choose, are taught to see the beauty in the enormous universe.

We get to wake up with the sun and sleep with the moon. We have 12-hours of light to make good in our day and 12 hours of dark to rest. Then to restart again as this world revolves.

Amazing isn't it?

We put our trust in this every day, hoping that we will awake to a new morning and start anew. Do we have a guarantee? Of course not! Do we get to choose how we use this day? Yes, we do. So I say, choose wisely.

Look at yourself every day in your mirror. See the beautiful person standing in front of you. What do you think? Only you know. Do you like what you see? Do you like how you feel? Change what you don't like. Only you can do this. Be your best you. Make your best you. Smile and smile again. Your eyes opened, this is for you, this is your choice. God said, "Good Morning."

33

Today is another amazing day. I woke up. I had no idea what today was going to bring. These last four days have been crazy. Complication after complication.

Dead batteries in S O's truck. My car died. I was stuck on the road, again. I was on my way to the dentist – emergency. S O had to come get me. S O and I both had a tooth problem. Mine was an ache. His implant fell out.

I had to leave my car on the side of the road, so now we were a few minutes late. I had my x-rays taken. Thank God it looks like my nerve in this tooth was angry, so now we watch it. S O gets his implant put back in. How it falls out is a mystery.

As I am waiting outside in his car, the sun is shining and I am praying. I am thanking God for my tooth, that it is not a major problem, at least for now. I am praying so that my car (a 1988 model) will only be a glitch. Bad fuel, or something easy. As I am telling God "please don't let this happen with my car again, it's just too much," S O comes out. He is finished and we proceed to my car on the side of the road.

Anxious that all will be okay and it will start. I hop in, turn the key and praise God, it starts Why? I can only say, "prayers," so I drive home. S O as well, and we begin our day of chores. This day of complications is not over, we need a new battery in the truck, but the easy fix will at least be manageable.

I sit and wonder why all at once those two vehicles at one time decide to break. The only thing that comes to my mind is, *slow down*. Stop being in a hurry. Time is here. Stop rushing. Okay...I'm trying.

We laugh at the complications and decide that things are not terrible. It could be worse. But *please*, not worse.

Get the battery, fix the truck. My car starts, I guess this corn gas is a problem, nothing that we can change, so deal. Make the day count. Everyone is healthy, everyone is alive. We can smile, laugh, breathe. All in all it's a good day.

34

A wonderful surprise comes in the mail today. A card from BF, saying thank you. As I read, she is being so generous with her words. She has read our/my book, "God Picked Me." Her kind words catch in my throat and choke me. Telling me how powerful these words on paper are. How they jumped off each page of telling my story. She said she enjoyed it so much that she is going to read it again. A little slower this time. Saying that through this book, this story has made an impact in her life. That I have made an impact. Thank you BF.

As I see it, God used me. I am always ready for God to use me...this human...to make whatever, impact or purpose for someone to be a child of our God.

I feel that is what this writing is all about. To put God's words, through me, on paper for others to read, hear and value. Thank You God. I know this is not only my story. It is God's words for this outcome, and God's love through these words, and God wanting to show that human life is not perfect, but through love of God and self, we together can help make this life a little easier to live. To be and try our human best every day. Yes, I do feel special to have been able to learn, listen and do as God has asked me again for a second time. I am writing another book. As God told me it would be called "THE ANGEL WITHIN."

35

I t is very early in the morning. Dawn is just arriving. The sky is beautiful, shades of pink through the heavens. Now I know why I am awake. I had to see this dawn and be brought back to my delight in God's world.

I had lost my way. It's the end of April and these days have been extreme. Attitudes have been on high. People have been tense. I allowed myself to fall into this trap, again. Covid-19, politics, celebrities, media, social casting. All of which I know better than to engage in. None of whom know what is going on in this world, God's world. I know better than to engage in this BS. I allowed myself to listen to reports, information, judgment, disrespect, and gossip. Again, I know better.

I felt the pull and yet didn't recognize the control of this human fault. God allowed me this time and gave me all I needed to pull me out. Finally I did, but to my behest, not fast enough. I've been up for hours, not being able to sleep. I'm finally beginning to understand why. I let this human world defeat me. I allowed all this distraction, confuse my mind. Dishearten my spirit. I know better. My inner being knows better. My human mind, body, self...forgot.

So now I've pulled back my balance and opened up my dysfunction to allow my inner peace to rule. Get to my place of calm and relaxation. Soak up my spirit and breathe. Yes, oh my, does this feel good!

Thank You God for teaching this human, me, these lessons on human nature. Thank you for calming the forces of evil and expelling them from me. Putting my mindset back into place.

Every day we are humans, we need to grow and use our "Angel Within" to our advantage. I forgot for a while, and I knew my balance was off. I let emotion carry me, and I was afloat. Not in a good way, but not totally awry. But knowing enough to know my kilter was off. Balance was needed.

At this time of confusion we are all a bit awkward. We are staying-at-home, and a bit stir-crazy. Understandable yes, but I/we can't allow this time to keep our balance off. We need to pull ourselves back and restart each day. Gather ourselves and claim our own. Easier said than to be done. Again...I know better.

I live through killing cancer. Many surgeries, colostomy, and reversal of colostomy. Yes, I know better.

I didn't hear God whispering to me, I blocked Him. On purpose? No...never! By my human error and not looking to the sky as I do. I lost my footing and tripped. I didn't fall, but I tripped.

Thank You God for catching me and holding me tight. I felt your arms and heard your tone. I awoke to choir music in my head and knew it was time to get my head clear and back to my sense of reality. God again "picked me" and I knew He was calling. How thankful am I to be able to hear this balance. To be able to be reclaimed into God's grace and feel His rescue. To be able to speak of this and put it to paper for all to read and claim for yourself. Yes, God has allowed me, his servant, to do His wish and inform all humans that they can and should be claimed by God. Ask Him, He will answer. As I have said many times, "God is calling," so answer.

My verse: "Come to Me with open arms, My arms will always be there,

Come to Me and hold Me tight, My arms will never fail."

36

Hello today, I need help, I'm in a gloomy place. I'm not feeling that great. My tummy is making me worry. As it is very tender and doesn't cooperate with the rest of my body many times. I ate too many vegetables, or too much salad, or fruit. I never know which one, or ones, is going to set it off. I've only been able to start eating many of these three food categories about six months ago. After my cancer surgery in 2017 and having my bowels reconstructed, this left me with a colostomy for 18 months. When it was finally reversed on October 22, 2018, I had to get my large intestine to gradually accept fruits, vegetables, and salads again. The process was slow and the attacks were brutal. I would have stomach problems that put me in diarrhea explosions. I never knew what would set it off, but I learned how to cope by going slow and moderate on days. Two days off and one day on. Then I could increase, until another explosion, and start again. It was a live and learn type of situation. Some were good weeks, some were not. But I prevailed and got through. Two weeks ago I had a very bad explosion and it was with me for days. It made me very nervous and I had cramping in my intestines for days. I hadn't had this for a very long time...months. But when this happens it brings me back to the beginning and my panic level soars. I'm hurting and have to be very careful as to what I put in my tummy, foodwise. Then there is the blood in stools. That's when my panic gets the best of me. Right away my mind goes into "CANCER" mode. Oh my it is coming back! Am I starting again? Do I need to be nervous? Everything a person could think of to put yourself into a panic. So, I know what to do. Watch it, chart the signs, make a note of what is happening and be on the alert. I hate this.

Since we are on Covid-19 and stay home, my appointment with Dr. A has been changed to June. Two months away. That scares me too! So I will chart and take notes to follow myself and be the best advocate for me. This doesn't mean I'm okay with this at all. Blood in your rectal area is not good. But it could be as simple as a hard stool that got pushed too much to come out or caused the tissue in the colon to be rubbed or scratched (the tissue is very tender and soft).

So my days are going to be wait and see. Eat normal, not too much soft or hard food, find the balance to produce easy stools. And yes, pray. Pray that God has my back and guides me through this trying time. Keep myself calm and let knowledge be my comfort. God has brought me through many trials and this is no different. I must be positive and controlled. Be vigilant and steadfast. So pray, I am and will. Thank You God!

37

Today I go back to Keytruda. Another three weeks of my immunotherapy drug to keep these cancer cells at bay. It is working. It is strange to have to wear a mask and protect myself and these wonderful nurses. They put their lives on the line for all of us, healthy or not, victims of cancer. Monday was bloodwork to check to see that all was good to get my treatment/infusion. So now we begin.

I saw Dr. S today as well. It's been awhile. He is a comfort in my life. We have been together since 1996. Wow, since my original bout with this cancer. Endometrial/cervical. We have been through a lot, and Dr. S has taught me so much about cancer, myself, my life, and how he has my best interest at heart for me to live. Information and understanding are blessings to this human body. Thank you Dr. S.

Now we move on to getting my PET scan and see how my internal body is performing. It's scary to know this is my life today, and at least for now. I'm alive, God's miracle, moving forward. Thank you Dr. S, see you in three weeks.

38

I hate politics. Why are these people we elected trying to use scare tactics? We are all in stay-home-mode. No jobs, no work, no...no...no! People are hurting. They think that the government will save us.

Oh my, people, the government does not save you! Nothing is free. You must work to provide for yourself and your family. PERIOD.

My prayer today:

Dear God, thank You for our world, thank You that we have free will. Thank You for us, humans, to be able to have minds that think, act, move, create. Show us Your mercy, grace and thoughts.

People are in need. We open our hearts to Your power, to greatness, and the mind You choose to show us our future. Thank You amen.

39

It's been another few weeks in the stay-home-life. Wear a mask, keep your distance, this is my space. Enough already!

I hope when God decides this event is over, that people see the harm and cruelty to human life we ourselves create. Earth, this world, was given out of love for our fellow man, created by God's grace.

When humans decide they are greater than God, when they decide not to follow God's rule, and instead follow man-made rules, we have a problem. "Man-made." Do you get that? Man has been taught to fight the rigors of establishment, and some things I will agree with. But to fight God and all He has created for our good, I don't get. Yes, we have free will. But to gather and manifest to manipulate. No, stop, think, listen, you are being sheep and are just like lambs going to slaughter. I know you can feel it in your heart. It is wrong and you want to break free. Do it, walk to the other side and say, *no more.*

God guides us, He gives us our minds to teach and learn. So use your mind for you. I have been saying this, and God keeps telling me to not be that lamb. Be the leader of the pack, be the shepherd, be the protector of the flock and recorder of these words. Human people please, I beg you, this time is here to bring awareness and comfort, not sorrow and pain, not panic and scare tactics. But rather to help us humans learn how to use our free will for the good of our human race. All humans, all monuments, all hearts. This is not love from God. This is the pride of mankind and power of fear. God doesn't put fear of logic into our hearts. God puts fear of truth in our free will to discern the truth of free will. Please open your heart, mind, body to the power of God through yourself. Be that shepherd of truth. Bring God's world back to God. Make your free will your power to discern for yourself and create your individual strength for our own logic and belief. Ask God to help you create this and watch how growth blooms within your body to reveal the strength within. You have the strength to create a mindset for you to be your best you. To guide your families to greater good through God and His wisdom.

I urge you to see and believe in your strength for yourself and all mankind. Be positive, be happy, be your God-given self. I know you can feel this in your heart. God bless you, all. Now is the time.

40

Today is PET scan day. 7:30 a.m. Mask on, standing and waiting my turn. I am the first for the day. Happy about that. Okay, radiation drug in my arm. Now to sit for 45 minutes. Done. Now, to lay on the table and enter into the tube for the 30-minute scan. Arms up over my head, lay still, don't move. In and out, back and forth. The test sounds. Pray, rest, calm. Yes, it's moving me out. It's over. Now to wait for a disc to carry home. Wait for the results to get to Dr. S, as I see him next Friday, Keytruda day. One day at a time.

This weekend is Mother's Day, May 2020. Happy Mother's Day to all moms. Enjoy.

41

Our life in Covid-19. Finally some loosening in this virus. We will be able to decide, as we choose to in some capacity, to stay home or go out. Life needs to open up more and the politicians have taken down some of our rules. Many people are going to be happy, many are not. Stage one - retail stores open, salons open, (I am one who is happy). People need to get back to a new normal and figure what this is going to be. We as humans need to decide our own future. Do you go or stay home? Breathe fresh air or continue to wear a mask and hinder your breath? Decide for yourself. But remember our lungs need fresh air. Without sun, air, breeze...we CAN'T live. Take your breaths, go out or stay home. Be your judge, your advocate, your choice. Be with people or be alone. Again your choice.

These times are new to some, and others have lived this before. Have we not learned our history? Have we not seen, or read about dictatorship. Have we blinded ourselves to the ongoing danger of repeating history?

Make yourself your part of this human life and open your mind to not repeat. Again and again. My mind keeps going back to, "give unto Caesar what is Caesar's, and give unto God that which is God's." Think about this sentence.

Caesar was money, taxes, rule...

God is human life given to mankind for love, peace, humanity.

Read to understand where you want to fit in. Do your due diligence for yourself and become your best advocate for you. Understand law, rules, choice. Pick your belief and consume your reality. Be kind, generous, gentle, steadfast. Breathe fresh, see beyond, hear nature, but always nurture your being you.

God has given us this beautiful land to prosper, grow, live. We need a time to recap our individual selves and decide who or where our being is going. Make your days complete with your goals, and achieve your greatness. Be positive, be gracious, be diligent, be successful. Be your best you. This is your choosing, your free will. Take these past weeks and arrange your daily life to fulfill your goals. Success is not things, it is balance within these things. We all work hard to achieve our goals and we enjoy doing it . So enjoy making this balance fit your life. Move forward, continue, grow along your path. Grow to know who you are, as well as where you are going.

These are God's plans and hopes for every human that has been graced by God's holy hands.

Use them to carry your human existence to meet your balance. Complete your ideals and grow your inner strengths. Be God's child of earth and fulfill your future .

Understand we have but one life, and we don't get to repeat our past. Move to a greater beginning, learning this balance and creating your purpose. Be good to yourself, not self indulgent. Be creative, constant, happy, smiling...be your best you.

42

This lesson and words came to me today.

"Life is about living through this pain, and learning how to deal through it."

This is how life is. Living and dealing. We will always have some kind of pain. Be it physical or emotional. What we must do is learn how to live and deal through it. We will always have this as a day-by-day challenge. Doing our best and completing each task is the how and through.

Be your best to you. Take this life and challenge yourself. Deal, and break through this pain. Every day. This is for you...

43

K eytruda, PET scan results, Dr. S day.

All went well. PET scan is clean, clear, no cancer, 28-months and cancer free. This is a happy day. Dr. S says scans are good and nothing to report. Now get Keytruda, 40 minutes, in and out. Solemn day here at the cancer center. Everyone is quiet and doing jobs. Okay, done. Have a great day all.

Amazing how things work out. I'm very happy with this process. Take care of me and move forward. Thank You God. You always teach me to look to You for clear thinking. Don't stress unless there is something to stress about and even then relax first, then breathe. Learn balance and one thing at a time. Each portion is its own entity. Each obstacle is its own hurdle. Yes, I can do this. Yes, I am in control. Yes, this too shall pass.

44

It amazes me when I awake each day not knowing if I will write or not. Today, I thought it would be a NO day. That was fine as it has been for a while.

Then I read an article as S O was still asleep and was intrigued.

This woman was apologizing to someone for being judgmental. I found her words encouraging. She took the time to apologize and it changed her thought process in the apology. As God works in all of us, it made my heart leap and feel happy. Using this letter to bring joy to my own inner feelings. Smiles, to her for her truth.

Then S O awoke, came, appeared in our kitchen. I told him about the letter. Read it to him, he smiled, and moved on to our morning. Thankfully he makes me cappuccino every day.

So many things going on, we always talk about them, and then move on to the weather. This spring season has been so different. The climate is cool, rainy, every day a new change. Yesterday was beautiful, sunshine, warm and you just wanted to be outside. This morning is rainy, windy and still warm, but you certainly don't want to be outside moving about. A typical spring day. As we were chatting, he said this spring has been up and down. No predicting what each day will bring. I agree. Then he said, "I can see why God is pissed." The weather, as we are at stay-at-home, has been keeping most from doing many things.

My heart leaped and we talked more on what I thought, as well as his thoughts, and I came to be very happy. This man, my S O and I, were on the same page. God granted us this communication to believe together. To feel in unison. Normally we are, but this gave my heart a special boost of confirmation. Thank You God. Again, today is a beautiful day.

45

It's mid June 2020. Summer is arriving. Warmth is as the sun shines on this beautiful world.

Many diversions, happenings, much anger, derogatory feelings, I won't go into this, except to say, "being angry, mean and cruel, is not acceptable." We are all human beings and need to respect each other's views of these times. "Not to repeat history."

God has given us our own thinking and knowledge to discern the ways of all . To keep ourselves in check and respect all areas of facts. I think at this point the rule of stop, think, breathe, is in great order. As God keeps reminding me we all are "The Angel Within".

46

I am so saddened by the events of today. Many problems to hear, see, acknowledge. Many would not be occurring if people accepted that they themselves are responsible for the actions they themselves produce. When are we going to get in our heads, "we reap what we sow." We are responsible for our own actions. We are our own responsible life partner. We need to accept responsibility for our own selves. We make the judgment call for what we encounter. It is our ownership. No one tells us, no one picks, no one demands our outcome, but we ourselves. We pick the things that we do each day. We decide to breathe, eat, sleep, move. We decide to be healthy, ignore, accept. We are our own decision-maker. That is called *choice.* We alone choose our day. We alone choose our outcome for every moment of our life. We make that yes-or-no decision. NOBODY makes this for us. WE ALONE ARE RESPONSIBLE. Do we get this ?

Nothing we do is FREE. There is a cost for everything. "NOBODY OWES YOU ANYTHING." We are humans. We breathe, we move, we decide, we accept. If you don't change you, you are the reason you are who you are.

DO YOU GET THIS ?

If you want something, earn it. Get a job, do a service. Earn your way. Thinking someone needs to pay for you is not how life is. Life is a choice. Choose wisely.

Again, "LIFE IS NOT FREE."

Yes, you are an individual, as you are meant to be. So be it. Be that one who is outstanding. Be that one to make your mark. Show your best, be creative, be your best you. Work hard, earn your way. We all have this ability within our being. How much do you want it? How much does it mean to you? Where are you going? Only you can decide your future. Only you can change for your own sake. You either want it, or you don't. Sounds easy, but it does take work.

Get good grades in school. Try your best. You have it in you. Find your encouragement and show yourself that you deserve it. It is about you, yourself, your decision. Taking the easy way is a choice. Thinking handouts are the only way leads to your not being satisfied. Fulfill your dreams. This is your choice.

You are responsible for you. You own it. Choose wisely, choose you.

47

Today God has me thinking. Oh boy. I had to realize I am a child of earth. I am a child of conscience. My life is my own. Many people have helped me to grow. Yes, grow. I also learned with their help, I became me. I learned the good, some bad, some just okay. My real lesson was, I learned ME. I made these choices to be ME. I took this responsibility to own who I am. I made these choices for myself, and I made me. I learned my lessons every day . A daily conflict goes on, but in the end I decided, I learned, I only. That feels great. Sure as a kid, we all have adults in our life. That is their job to try and teach. As an adult I did the same. Teach the young. As I sometimes did, and sometimes I didn't. As an adult sometimes I taught and sometimes I didn't. As it all fell back to me. I own who I am. I made these choices to be who I am. NO ONE Forced me to be. NO ONE decided for me. I did it .

Wow, that is hard. It is, was, hard, learning to discern, good, bad, yes, no. Always my decision. My mistakes are mine. My challenges are mine. My accomplishments are mine. I am okay with this. I know I worked hard to be who I am. I know my heart. I know my dreams. I own my outcome. Things were not easy. They had complications attached. Some I created, some I let happen, some I gave in to. But all in all, I own it. Again it's all okay.

I am living it now and changing some. I learned better. I accept my own decisions. I am grateful. Lessons take time, understanding, encouragement. That alone is a lesson and a learned one. Yes, I'm still learning, and I love it. We all are humans, we will never stop learning. We need to allow ourselves to learn and accept that it is necessary. Learning is growth. Learning is an accomplishment. Learning is love.

So I ask, do you love to learn? Do you love yourself enough to keep learning? Yes, I am sure you do. So keep learning.

God wants me to share my lessons, my thoughts, my dreams. Yes, God's power. Use God to power you. Use God to encourage you. Use God to teach you. Let God's lessons be a guide to your life. Allow God to be your lesson in your life. God always finds my higher power and makes me go higher. This is truth to me. Without God in my heart, mind, and life, I know I would be empty.

I love my humans. I love their knowledge, lessons, encouragement. Everything they bring to my life. One thing that is so steady for me is that I know no matter what I do, what I see, what I ask, God is my power of truth. My heart feels it. My mind knows it. My life reflects it. Thank You God for loving me and showing me how to love You. Every day, all day, I look to God. My answers are always through God. He heals me. He teaches me. He allows me to be me. He accepts me. He loves me.

I will always do this, as I have done all my life. At times when I was younger, I knew God was there, but my young mind could not comprehend this. As I learned and understood, it was always very clear. It was God's way to show me, to have me learn, to have me understand. Yes, I know this now. Thank You God.

Yes, again, God has me thinking. So today I think, and I am thankful that I can. Thank You God.

In all your ways acknowledge Him, and He shall direct your paths. (Proverbs 3:6)

48

So many messages come to me. It scrambles my mind at times. I tried to remember them all, but I know I can't. Being protective is harder than I think. I understand all will not be revealed at once. It takes time for our human mind and body to comprehend all. I do wish all was instant. Things come in as they should for the message to be clear. We get the timing perfect for each message.

Some take days, some weeks, some in bits and revealing the whole in months. I've had this many times, and boy, when it is complete it is very powerful, understood and clear. God in His perfect knowledge gives us humans that exact time and course we need to accept these truths. I so love when all gets explained and I understand His timing. It is PERFECT.

When we become closer to God, understanding His power for our life, we comprehend His value in us. We become His prophet to bring words, lessons and messages to many. Those that want to be will know. Those that know will understand. Those that want will also bring messages. Who your God is, is not everyone's God. We are all of different faiths . Bottom line is, God is your power in many mighty messages. All are good. Messages provide your knowledge to help others bring knowledge as the circle goes around. All have the message to be learned, shared, understood, accepted. This is how God shows His love for us and we show our love for God.

Take a moment. Breathe, listen, hear, let your mind rest in the knowledge. The message you know is waiting for you. Pass it on. Give it strength. Put the words to the message.

Yes, I know you know what I am talking about. Enjoy this and smile. Happy smiles. Today starts a new message. "God Picked Me."

49

W hat is so beautiful about waking up early in the morning, is the silence. The quiet. Everything is still. Everyone is still asleep. The noise is nil. Sounds echo because of the calm of the beginning of a new day.

As I am awake, God has me again thinking of why silence is so important. Yes, the word silence, its meaning.

Silence: A noun: complete absence of sound. The fact or state of abstaining from speech

A verb: cause to become silent, prohibit or prevent from speaking.

Silence: many times in our lives we must or have been made to be silent. Many reasons for silence. Prayer, a speech, church, sorrow, conversations, sleep, meditation, gratitude, scolding...a long list. As I am reflecting on why silence is important. I remember to understand the many reasons why it is needed for importance. Learning is silent. Reading can be silent. Understanding is silent. Respect is silent.

In God's nature of silence all things become alive after the silence. As we bed down after a long day we get to silence. Sleep. Then start anew the next morning as we begin again.

I am not sure I really ever gave silence the thought to understand how important this word, this being, this stage of silent life is. Many times my silence has gotten me through a period of need. Many times silence has brought me comfort. Keeping quiet. Many times not being silent, has brought me pain. So as I reflect on me and understand my own word silent, or silence, I begin to see why God is pushing me to understand this meaning.

Our world, this world, needs more silence. During this pandemic time, I get this silence. God is teaching us humans to stop and hear the silence of today. We humans need this. We humans have to understand this. We humans must do this. Our bodies need silence. We require this to rest our own being and to calm emotion, stress and outrage. We keep putting ourselves in overload. Do you see this? Can you accept this? Do you want to change this?

I am trying to move forward to bring a new balance to my silence. I have learned to be less loud, to not be quick to speak, to not jump at every fraction of disappointment. To remember concerns of being happy, smiles, defeat, wellness, hope, many emotions. As God says, silence.

I hope this moment of silence has given you a pause to rethink, reflect, reboot your own silence. As it is said, "Silence is Golden."

50

As I was sleeping and began to awake today God spoke to me and reminded me about trust. Oh my, I'm in for it now.

Today trust is such a big thing, word, completion. I do not trust easily. I guess I could say many have broken my trust and now I don't give it easily. To me, trust is something that is given, and you must keep earning to be able to keep it. In my stages of trust, a person must show trust through many aspects. Loyalty, love, generosity, kindness, respect, knowledge, and many more. The list is long. I have faltered. I have broken. I have abused trust, as we all have, making fools of ourselves in the process. Trust is so special, and yet we break these trust. Sometimes never knowing we can't get it back. Yes, I have done it. I have, and I now reap the disaster of losing that trust. I also have had many do this to me. So I know how it feels. Most of the time when trust is broken, it is not given back. This is understandable. Other times, when a trust is broken, and you do give it back, you become the trust. You set the boundaries. You are the giver. This I have done also. Then there are the times when no trust is allowed. You made your effort and trust is not received, and it is broken again. Not to be given back. You learned a very hard lesson on why or how and you must walk away. Trust hurts. Yes, when a trust is broken and reflects on the giver or the taker, it always hurts.

I know we all have had trust become a hurt. A disappointment. Even a disaster. People do this every day. In our personal life, our job, our relationships, even with God. I am guilty of this. I have had to repent. I have had to accept this. I also hate that it is a part of my past, present and future. Hoping to realize before it manifests to un-trust. But, this is the truth. So I must accept my part.

God is showing me that all trust is not bad. That trust is beautiful. How to trust. How to accept. How to show how trust works. Yes, I trust God. Yes, I have my trust. I have people whom I trust. I have people whom I do not trust.

In God's infinite wisdom, He has taught me to be a more trusting, trustworthy, trust giving human. I am glad to know, and to be able to work on this every day. It doesn't mean I allow everyone to gain my trust. It doesn't mean that everyone trusts me. Trust is a work in progress.

As I mature and understand the boundaries of trust, it is a working part of life. Trust becomes love, emotion, and comfort. Trust is passion, understanding, knowledge. I am so thankful for being able to discern where to place my trust in this life. God has given me this as a daily reminder to be a better me, and be full of trust. Thank You God.

51

It is a beautiful summer day. The sun is shining, the sky is blue, the clouds are fluffy. Yes, it is a beautiful day.

Weeks have been flying past, time is speeding by. I need to slow down and smell the roses. My sleep has been uneasy. I keep waking up at 5 a.m. Arrrrrrr! I know God is preparing me for a new chapter. I feel like I am moving up, up, up. My thoughts are racing. I don't want to miss the next step.

As God has done in the past, I feel He is preparing me for a new reality which will come to light. I don't have any idea what it is, but I know it is coming.

Yes, God, I am ready. Yes, God, I am looking . Yes, God, I am open. One thing I do know, as I have been prepared before, God's timing is perfect, complete, and just. So I will be aware, conscious, and waiting for God's revelation.

52

ENCOUNTER #6
June 1, 2020

I dreamt I was asking, "What is going to happen?"

Was I hearing correctly?

"History will repeat itself" again and again.
I asked "Is it the Holocaust?" The answer was "NO, NO, NO."

I woke up.

S.O. Heard me yelling.

As we are seeing. it is about our time of riots, killing, and unrest. People are repeating the times of chaos, burning, and destroying. God help us.

53

ENCOUNTER #7

June 8, 2020

My dream: I was with family members, at a mosaic shop in a house. It had all types of marble carvings, statues, animals, and people. I felt very uncomfortable, like it was somehow evil. All of a sudden I was holding a plaque with the image of the Blessed Mother Mary on it. Beautiful in color and moving. She was speaking to me.

Mother Mary told me everything will be alright. To go and look for a wrought iron pole and climb on. As I did, the pole was made with crosses all over it. It was beautiful. So I stood on it and it lifted me up in the air onto the roof and placed me down. I got off and felt the relief of being comforted by God. Peaceful now, I woke up.

Now as I am looking back upon this encounter. I realize it all had to do with the way people are perceiving the statues of today. The way they are tearing them down. Dishonoring our history of yesterday, today and tomorrow.

Yes, this is evil, as I am feeling, "Oh my God, please help us." God thank you for granting me, this human, your knowledge of today and the ability to use your words.

54

When I think of the past few weeks, I am reminded of all the keywords I have used, and the reasons for them.

Trust, Truth, Silence, Facts, Responsibility.

Each one has so much to learn, remember, listen to and keep in our vocabulary. These words are necessary for our everyday life. When you don't speak the TRUTH, it is a LIE.

When you don't have TRUST, you have anarchy, uneasiness.

When you don't have SILENCE, you can't hear, learn, or understand.

When you don't have FACTS, you cannot trust who or what is telling the truth. How to be in SILENCE.

Understand all to be known of the FACTS.

Then take RESPONSIBILITY for you.

As God has shown and proven, these words are the foundation in our world. We need to be honest with ourselves and figure out how to make ourselves the creator of our own life. We need to be responsible for every day, every action, every word.

Take responsibility for you.

Do you see how you are the only one who can claim these words for yourself, your being, your life, your future. Come on people realize this. Accept this. Change for the better. Make yourself that star that shines bright so all can see the best you.

55

Lately I am reading, working, and listening to all these messages coming through from many sources to find the most correct information I can.

Not only are so many contradicting each other, but you just don't know who is speaking the truth. Yes I say, *truth*. Reports are misleading and either give you only what you, (as they think) need to be told, or half truths and misspeak about the message. How to discern the complete projection of what is being said. I'm confused. So I must turn to God for the perfect understanding of all this. I do know that in time I will have all the understanding of the facts and be given the true meaning. Why is it, in the great expanse of this world, people are so misleading. What happened to the idea that the human mouth should be true when it speaks. What happened to the concept of using exact words to get the message of what happened.

The idea of being correct, truthful, and honest. You almost have to be a mind reader to get the correct information and discern the messages being spoken. In many things I don't want to have to be that interested to get to the bottom of a mundane message. Many messages are not worth understanding. It's not necessary to have to put so much effort into this type of information. It angers me to have to do this. It's so simple, when people just give the facts truthfully and make the message complete the first time. Instead everyone puts their own spin on the message. They sensationalize it to be broader and misleading. They think it makes bigger and better reporting. I'm sorry, I disagree. I can't stand this type of reporting anymore. So I do my own fact checking and look further for the correct information. Has it taught me a few things? Yes, it has. Has it stopped me from listening to these half truths? Yes, it has. Am I better for it? Yes, I am.

I guess it's always been this way. Find your own knowledge in what is being said so you will not be misled or misguided by someone's else's words. Someone else's input, someone else's bias. It is so frustrating. I am sure you agree. But this is today and these times. So we either do our own best for ourselves, or we allow others to do it for us. I choose not to be the lazy one, but to encourage all to do their own seeking. Choose to become a more informed person, to the betterment of yourself. Be correct, clear, and precise.

Always put yourself up to the challenge to be truthful in your words, actions, and messages.

Ask God to show you. He will, you know. He does, you will see. Be open to this truth and you'll find you are the one who always comes up with the truth of a conversation.

56

I guess it is so true, and it keeps getting worse. If you want to be misunderstood write a text.

Nobody wants to talk anymore. Everyone wants things in a text, email, or in a darn computer. I really dislike computers. Of course you have to use one in this day and age. But it doesn't mean you have to *like it*.

Things get so misconstrued, mislabeled, mis-worded. Oh, and then there is spell check, and they used the wrong words. Not you, but the darn computer. Seriously, the computer doesn't like your sentence so they correct it to what they want it to say. REALLY? NO!

I'm so disgusted!

Today, yesterday, and maybe tomorrow!

People, stop putting words where they don't belong and putting your own value on someone else's words. I don't like it, and I'm sure you don't either. Say what you mean, or don't say anything.

Confusion plus.

God has taught me, more words are better. Spell it out. In words, less is NOT more. I try my hardest to not be misunderstood. If you don't understand, ask a question. Don't automatically think you know my thoughts. Do you know what ASSUME means? YES!!

Everyone is so quick to judge each other. Stop it. Take a breath, breathe, think.

God, I ask for Your help. I need to discern. To balance. To connect. It's lost and I want mine back.

Everyone is taking things out of context. Thinking they know more about what you are saying than you do. Always interrupting, putting a spin on these words and making them their own. Please tell me why, the word needed here is *listen*. Try understanding, be part of the conversation, not the conversation. It's getting harder every day as many want what they want, and don't care about the other. It's out of control. Again, less is not more in some of these situations. Do you get that? Do you see that? Do you understand this? Well, we all need more words, understanding, and communication. Stop being so selfish, and listen more.

God hears, sees, and understands everything. Maybe we humans need a lesson in this. To be better listeners and better hearers, rather than interpreters.

Do you get it? Well, at least we humans need to try harder.

I've said this before, and I will say it again. Listen please. Don't interpret. Be patient. Hear with your ears, not your mouth or your words. Maybe some of the anger will stop. Maybe some of the energy will be understood. Maybe some of the message will be heard.

My prayer for today:

Please God help me to be a better listener and learner. To hear, rather than to interpret, all the words from my humans daily. Thank You God, Amen.

57

Chemo got me again.

By that, I mean it's been almost 3 years since my last chemotherapy session. The last of my eight injections of poison running through my body, veins, and internal organs. I knew this day would come again. As cancer is in your body, you must have chemo to kill the cancer in your body. That is great and needed. But the aftereffects of chemo, normally years later, come back in ways to harm you. Again it's okay. You are alive and moving forward. We are told it could happen. Not all will have it, but we could. My aftereffect came to my mouth, my jaw bone, and my teeth. All was fixed in 1996 after my first bout with cancer and chemo, 1995 into 1996. So today again my aftereffect is my teeth. Some are dying and or dead.

Today is pull-the-tooth day. I am losing another tooth. In 2015 it was an upper molar. Today it's a bottom molar. Chemo kills all cells that your body generates. It doesn't pick between the good or bad, it kills all. The possibility of having a problem may, and with me does occur. In me it's my teeth. Thankfully something can be done. Just pull the bad one out and decide how to move forward. Maybe an implant, or maybe leave it alone. That is down the road, as the damaged, dead must be removed now. So today is pull-the-bad tooth out. Get the body to heal and another time decide what is next. Thank You God.

58

Today is rainy. Day after tooth extraction. I'm writing. My tooth is out. I'm exhausted, swollen, and sore. It took over an hour to extract. In sections, cleaned, and eight stitches later, I'm good.

Day three. Cheek and chin, black and blue, still swollen and sore. But I am okay. This too shall pass. Slept okay. Thank God for pain medication. All is good. It's just a tooth. The least of all that could have been affected by chemo. In my gut I knew this would happen. Better to be toothless than to have my heart or kidneys affected. So I'll take it. Thank You God.

59

ENCOUNTER #8

July 23, 2020

The most amazing thing happened today. I've been searching and praying for this picture, or cover of this book, to appear. Today my prayers have been answered. It came to me in a strange way as far as human standards are concerned. God always has the perfect settings, timing, ways...

"The Angel Within" has a cover. It's perfect. God has given His approval. God made this happen.

Thank You God, Amen.

60

Life is a lesson we all learn. Acceptance is a power. Live to the fullest and never look back. Forward is our gain.

WOW, This came to me and made me realize that we all, whether we want to or not, must be part of every day. Learn, seek, believe and accept. We all must accept our own responsibility. I know I keep saying this, but it's an every day method we must live by, accept and be responsible for.

This reckless world today has not been about acceptance of our own. We have said, "it's your fault, not mine." We have given into "not me, you." Oh people, do you see the trouble this has caused? If we learn nothing else, please learn, we all own our own destiny. We own our own lives. We own our own tomorrows. No one else is responsible, except we ourselves.

God asks, God expects us to be our best us, for us. God shows forgiveness and understanding, and love. God gives compassion, humanity, and respect. Are we living these things? Do we reciprocate back to God and others?

Please find it in your heart to cleanse yourself. To bring yourself forward, forget the past, move to a new beginning. God is love. So love you, love them, love all. Thank You God, Amen.

Do you see how bitterness has broken the world...our world? Do you see how greed has become of value today? Do you understand the meaning of sharing? Do you understand that taking what is not yours is stealing?

I'm trying to give facts to you to help you to see that you are owed nothing, except what you earn. You earn respect, you earn a salary, you earn a home, you earn loyalty, you earn grace, you earn love, you earn value. You earn manners, you earn support, you earn everything you have, every day. If you don't earn it, how did you get it?

Please believe me, you will love yourself more when you EARN, than if things are handed to you for free, or if you take what belongs to someone.

God has asked us to earn our way to heaven. To be and know true self for the good of self. Is this a part of your everyday life? Do you earn you? Do you earn today? Do you earn respect?

I do hope your answers are: "YES GOD, I DID EARN. Be kind, be happy, be you....

61

I am still in a chill zone. These past few weeks are sometimes more than I want to remember. This poor world we live in. People are not, or choose to not be, human. All this chaos and destruction. Don't we realize we are hurting the structure of the economy? When personal property is destroyed it hurts everyone. These businesses and hard-working people's livelihood are a part of economic strength. Tearing this down does not help our foundation. Destruction doesn't help us to hear your cause or help your credibility. Violence begets violence. Strength is not shown through violence. Wanting to be heard is not achieved through violence. This is chaos. Only chaos. I wish people could see beyond this and realize the platform of these wrongs. God help us, help us all.

I've had to say goodbye to three different people in the last few weeks. Not easy, but I hope they are in God's rest and strength. May you rest in peace and find glory, amen.

We never know who or what will cause a light in someone's life to go out. Be it illness or "I'm done," or other situations. By the will of someone or the will of our own, it happens.

We try to teach ourselves to hang onto the light the best we can and to do our due diligence for ourselves.

We only have one life we must live to our own full strength. To take pride in ourselves and teach ourselves how we need to be the best human possible. This is a true reality for our being. Hurting others and taking from them will not be to our benefit during our lifetime. Trying to work together usually is good for all. This doesn't mean it always works, sometimes it doesn't. So you have to walk away. As walking away is not a bad thing either. Sometimes it saves you. It balances you. It gives you the strength to move forward. It is not your responsibility to restore all. We know we cannot, but remember you, your balance, always wants to move forward and holding back only holds you back from your forward and your balance. These lessons I can tell you I have had to learn many times. It is okay to bring your balance, and to walk away in order to move forward. Think for you. Think for you forward, balance, safety, strength. Nothing is not for you. You own your own. Move for you and it is always forward.

62

Different forces are moving forward. Things are changing every day. While the sun does always shine, and the moon always has its glow, the world around us is every day changing.

Our goal is how we change with it. Are we the individual we want to be, or do we conform to follow the sheep. This is, and will be, a personal struggle. I see it happening. Our generation is holding tight to what used to be, as we know it. Our generation is branching out. Some to better, others to followers. God created us all to be individuals. We have different skin color, hair color, eye color. What we do have as one, is our bodies. They are all the same on the inside. All have the same organs to live. We have a brain, heart, lungs, etc. Not one of us is different in this respect. So what about our outside. Why is it such a problem for many to dislike? As I am taught, individuality is good. It is important, it is supreme in being. Do you understand this? God created us all equal. Some are skinny, some are fat, some are tall, some are short. But your internal body is all the same. We must remember that. We all have a heart to discern how we want to be beating daily. Do we beat for good? Do we beat for evil? Only you with your brain, your thoughts, can make this beating heart your Captain. Your heart always tells you of your decision. When your heart hurts, you know it is wrong. When your heart goes numb, you know the trouble you are in. When your heart says NO, and you do YES, you know you made that mistake. I urge you to listen to your heart more and understand it's a beating, living, organ to teach you to be the best you.

Every day, all day, by God's grace, discern for you and do your best. Ask God to help. God will and does show you, us, all. Thank You God.

63

Weeks, months, almost a new year. Time is moving closer to becoming a new year. By the end of summer, as it's around the corner, time for many revelations to be in play. Keeping eyes open, seeing, you can keep you in tune. Learn as much as you can. Be optimistic about what you hear. Be prudent in what you do. Remember you are the leader of you. Be diverse in your actions, show when you are different, you have a variety of skills. Be majestic, not overbearing, kind, cool, calm. And yes, smile.

Things will and are changing. We may not like what is before us. As long as we are prepared, we will have accomplished much. Take the time you need to do you. To understand your surroundings, thoughts, being. The time is now to be your best you. Graduate into a beautiful creature of purpose. Define your person. Your skill set. I'm hearing all these words about following the crowd. Please don't. Be you. Be confident in you. Protect you. Grow you. Please you, always be you.

Follow your design, your plan, your identity to be you. We are not the sheep to be led to the field to graze. We are humans with brains, a mind and heart. Feel you. Seek that impact you desire.

I'm saying this as much to myself as I am you. Grow in spirit as well. Trust your instincts, your motivation, yourself. These are very important for this time of living in our, your, life. Open your eyes to the realization before you, and decide for you. The time is coming,

The time is now. This plan has been set. Do not underestimate yourself for your betterment. Courage will move you forward. Balance will keep you straight, move forward. Take those extra steps and you will see how good it feels to do so. I encourage you...move forward.

Try it, like it, do it.

God is calling, answer His call. Hear His words, His wisdom. Reflect on His presence. See the beyond. Look and seek, You know it's there. Find your way. Free your spirit, your mind, your being. As always, SMILE, yes always SMILE. Grace yourself. For God is preparing us. Be prepared.

64

W hen I think I have it all okay and something brings me to a halt. I must remember "The Angel Within," and the amazing power to prevail. This world is working in the presence of a great power. Beyond anything we can imagine. "God is the Power Beyond." People, do you get this?

"GOD IS THE POWER BEYOND"

Believe, pray, look up and see. Yes, you can see. Your heart tells you and you feel it. No demand is too hard for God. No condemnation is too hard for God. No persecution is too hard for God. Praise God, praise God. All who know have the strength, the being, the power for God to be. We do and will. Our prayers and love of God make it so. Our saying His name makes a truth. Our belief is our knowledge. Have knowledge in God and be His strength, for human life here on earth. Scream to the heavens His Holy name. Rejoice in the calm. Let your heart breathe in the solace. Remember who you are in this everlasting joy.

"God is the Power Beyond," keep saying it. God has spoken and told me these truths. Thank You God.

65

We all have a job to do. Live our life to the fullest. To be that creation of love, peace, joy. How do we do this? Have you thought about this? Do you understand how all this began?

This is the goal for every human on this earth, to be a better you. Our minds are for us to learn, To comprehend the knowledge that we grow up to learn and to understand the universe and the everyday aspects of our being. As always, learning to deal with the good, the bad and the misunderstood lessons. Not one man is our leader. Only God is our leader, this creator of heaven and earth. We are not to be ruled by a single human. We are to be taught by many humans, we are given lessons in every walk of life to retain knowledge and to be our own single-minded authority. We gain by being taught, but we live by understanding. We each have our own discernment with this knowledge. When spoken to, we retain. Then we go beyond and teach others. This is called: the history of being. To pass along important teachings to the generations after us, and so it goes, on and on. Always leaving an imprint of knowledge for future generations to come. When teachings are destroyed, forgotten, a new balance must occur. God gives, as well as takes. Remember Noah. This great land was being abused by human fault, destroyed by human greed, manipulated by human madness. The result was to wash away and start again.

Has man learned by this? Has human life begun this track again? God is our universal creator and master of this and all generations. We are headed toward the creation of change, a power struggle, the good versus the bad. Do you feel this ongoing "man against man?" God is in the thralls of the unbalance of our creation and will do the ultimate change, and to better our understanding and go beyond, to get human attention to bring us, humans, to the reality of balance. When balance is off, it tips and falls. So the equilibrium has to be put back to bring a pure balance. Equal balance. To sustain to be level. We must work on this in our daily life too. We know this, as we would not be able to stand without balance, to walk, hold ourselves up. Do you understand this? So how do you think the earth can go further without fixing this imbalance.

Think for yourself to know where your imbalance is. Bring balance back to you. You are in control of your own balance. Take this moment and find your balance to be level again. I know you understand, and I know you are knowledge-minded to do your work. Listen to your mind. Not the mind of another. No one can tell you what you're thinking. You have the power to move and propel yourself forward. Think and reason within you. Bring you, your teachings, and your understanding to the forefront. Do not allow you to be misled for another's result. This life is about you. Your challenges. Your balance. Your achievements. Your goals.

66

When people ask me why I feel the way I do, I tell them, the only way through this life is through God. You may think all this is because of you, but in reality it is what you choose and how you choose it. We make our own destiny. We possess a free will. As I have found my only way with my destiny is choosing to hear God within me and asking for His perfect result for me. I am a cancer survivor, not once, but three times.

I've lost my hair three times and it returned. I've had deadly chemotherapy three times. I'm still alive. I had major surgery, three times, and God gave me the strength to survive all of them. Not to say my doctor's hands of God's power worked these miracles. Yes I am that miracle...

As we are seeing so much tragedy in today's society, it doesn't surprise me that God is releasing so many miracles. The greed, the self-righteousness, the anger, and the hate, are all being allowed. Yet, all the power in prayer is overpowering these atrocities. These allowances in our daily life. People are seeing miracles every day to bring joy to them, and to realize that without God nothing can survive through the endless struggle of everyday life. God is our power, God is our joy, God is our praise, God is our Savior. God will and does bring peace. When your heart tells you, you know the truth. You realize the energy. You feel happiness, joy, commitment, rest. Yes rest in the joy of knowing God is in your heart. Feel that excitement that jumps for joy. As you do know where it came from, our God, our Creator, our divine power, God.

Do *you* every day. But also do *you* knowing the positive power through God that gives you this power to exist every day through God. Yes, I do. Yes, I believe. Yes, I am that miracle.

67

Loving oneself is a daily challenge in these troublesome days. We all need to find that moment to do this for us and others. Love hurts, and complains, it stings our being. As our hearts propel us forward to show that comfort through love. A hug, a kind word, a touch, that look, can bring a smile where a frown has been. People are set off by the simplest things to be angry and speak a challenging word. Think before you speak the word of anger. Let it mellow before the tone of change gets in your throat and becomes sound . Nobody wins in a war of words. When you say your words, make them truth, and don't slant the truth. Say what you mean, and understand that meaning before you speak. Words are weapons that can leave a scar. Challenge yourself to be better at this. I know, we all have done this. As we think about it, it makes more of a challenge. But this challenge is easier to accept than that of which we speak. Kinder is better, kinder is more joy, kinder is quieter. Be that kinder person to be a better you. Bring a gentle tone along and see the magnitude of you become soft. Your whole being will jump for joy at this tiny spark of change.

Allowing oneself to manifest the knowledge of mastering kindness brings forth change. Be that change for yourself, for all, for your betterment. Bring this together and see how many, if not all people will look, see, and perform this change. As one starts others follow. Be that one. Be that one who encourages this change. Be the start to bring change through you. Your words. Your smile. Your kindness.

Show to them this loving spirit to bring change to all. God is watching. He knows who will do this work. God reminds us and pushes us forward towards being that one who is loving. Show how God has used you, your words, your knowledge, for the betterment of all human hearts and words of comfort for this human race. Be a part of the love and peace . As you do, you will see and feel to bring the change for yourself, your own being. This is a better solution for today and every day. Our world needs this and is crying for this change. Pray for us, for a change in our being and peace will arrive through all the kindness of change. Thank You God.

68

Today I go back again to Noah. God keeps reminding me about Noah. Noah was a man, a human, a father, a husband, a lover of God. Noah, as God asked, did what was asked. Followed God's plan, made the ark, took all animals, two by two. Each kind, every species, all living, good, bad, kind, deadly. He built rooms for all these majestic animals to be on the ark. Stories tell of how the animals relied on Noah to bring them to a new land to prosper. They multiplied and became many over time. Do you see the understanding in this? Creatures were given the acceptance to go, Move on, grow and multiply.

Concerning humans, only Noah, his wife and family were allowed on the ark to restart human life again.

This day and time remind me of the days of Noah. We are becoming like those wiped out by the flood. We have become the "MIME," the "ME," this selfish generation. I'm saddened by this. We are not allowed to go and take from one another. We are not allowed to destroy one another's property. We are not allowed to steal from one another. It is not acceptable to burn another's property.

We need to wake up and see the destruction being caused. When did we lose our priorities?

When did we lose our truth? When do we lose our responsibility and respect for each other?

I know in my heart there are always going to be those ones who are unhappy, and who feel dissatisfied. But I also believe in my heart that we can be changed to see and realize the difference. We do this every day. We humans have this capability to change another's outlook. To show and teach those who are lost. To care to bring others to see great and beyond. This happens every day. We read about it. We see it. We do it.

A kind word. A kind gesture. A kind deed. Help is always just in front of us. When we see someone's pain, we lend our hand. We say that kind word. We all have done this and we all have experienced it. Giving or receiving. It has been there. We all have talked about that gesture to someone, whether given or received. We have explained what we saw or what we felt.

We have smiled or cried, but the fact is we share this experience with another. You see this is what makes us human. Caring, feeling, and seeing all this kindness, and then telling someone else. Let us keep the kindness going. Let us keep the smiles on every face. Let us keep the gestures moving forward for all this human race to continue. Let us show our love to every human, and let every human show it back to us again.

Be the change for today. Be the energy for today to start anew. As God loves us. Let us love others. Thank You God.

69

It was a beautiful September evening. My friend called me to tell me that what God had said to him through me, came true. He was so happy to be able to bring this information back to me with joy. Yes, my heart leapt. I reminded him, I was just the vehicle God used to bring this message to him.

We talked and he asked if I would autograph a few of my books for him. He said that he would like to pass them on to his friends. We got together and the signing was done. He was so glad I would stop and do this, no questions asked. As I feel "OUR" book "GOD PICKED ME" is to be out in this world for all. Signing is God's way of confirmation that a human person, "ME," was used for other humans. I do not take credit for these truths to be put to paper for my gain. This is work, yes, but work I am ready to perform daily, As God asked me once, and now again, being twice. I am very proud to put words to paper for all good to bring forth God's words with wisdom. How can I not? I am HIS miracle and was asked to perform this deed.

I was, and am, grateful for every day that I breathe. Writing is just a part of my daily breathing.

It makes me, a mere human, very happy to do this work. I am also glad many understand how I feel about the time and energy to be put toward this work. Thank you my loved ones. Your patience and strength helped me to write book #2. I love you all for this, more than you know. Again, thank you.

God has also told me that this work is not finished. When I had encounter # 6, February 14, 2020, at the end "Trilogy" was put on the paper. Knowing trilogy means three, I am ready for book #3. Thank you for using me, for allowing me, this work for my God.

To be continued...

ENCOUNTER # 9
September 2, 2020

As I was dreaming, God woke me and again, as many times before, had me write:

> "To encourage is to believe that God brings forth faith to promise those who believe everlasting peace, through love, guidance, and strength." Yes, "THE ANGEL WITHIN."

71

A friend's loving words to his partner:
How will you know love?

With just a touch

It will dispel loneliness with a whisper,

It will bring comfort out of grief,

It will heal anger and despair,

It will triumph over fear and hate,

It's the calm you are given when the storm is around you,

It's finding happiness in even simply sharing a glance or a
smile, It's the joy in the most trivial moments together ,

and support in the most difficult of tribulations.

How will you know love?

It's by doing all of this for another.

Thank you J.N. and P.M. for allowing this poem...

GOD

God, Angel, Me , to human.....

As this TRILOGY began.......

book 1   "GOD PICKED ME"

book 2   "THE ANGEL WITHIN"

book 3   ?

MEET THE AUTHOR

BONNIE J. SCHAAL, is a 3-time cancer survivor. She has known trials, tribulations, tragedy, truth. Her main goal in life is to bring forth words of love, wisdom, truth, from God to her, to be shared with all. She is a mom, a lover, a friend, a believer in God's Word. To be able to do this is the blessing only God could give.

Bonnie in various stages of recovery.